To my grandchildren now and those yet to be born. May your world be free from terrorism, discrimination, and bullying...

MASCOT BOOKS

www.mascotbooks.com

Barnyard Bully

For more information, please contact:
Mascot Books
560 Herndon Parkway #120
Herndon, VA 20170
info@mascotbooks.com

Library of Congress Control Number: 2016903212

CPSIA Code: PRT0616A
ISBN-13: 978-1-63177-024-1

Printed in the United States

Barnyard Bully

Dawn Marie Thompson

Illustrated by Oana Cochea & Anna Benczedi

The sun rose over the meadow, and the silhouettes of two horses stood in the distance.

Blaze and Buttercup grazed, taking in the first rays of sunshine that warmed them from the cool, spring night.

A truck pulling a trailer skirted up, and a painted horse was led down a ramp into the meadow.

Blaze and Buttercup looked at the new horse, and Blaze wiggled his lips and spouted, “You’re a horse of a different color. You don’t belong in this meadow!”

“What difference does it make what color I am on the outside? We are all the same on the inside!” said the new horse.

“I’m not sure I like someone different,” blurted Buttercup.

“You go graze over there,” she razzled, pointing her nose to the left.

The painted horse, whose name was Skylark, plodded to the left side of the meadow. “I don’t like being pushed around because of how I look. Boy, Blaze is such a bully!” Skylark said.

He hung his head, and his mane covered his eyes.

Over at the hen house, the hens were all perched on high. With their necks craned out, over, and down, they waited for the talk of the town…or at least, the barnyard.

"Where did you hear that?" one gaggled.

"Oh, did you hear this one?" another one gasped.

They pecked and talked, pecked and talked,
talked and pecked.

"Did you hear what…?" a third chimed in.

She was interrupted by the wide-eyed gaze of Chelsea, the chicken across from her. She turned her neck slowly and looked to see what Chelsea was staring at, only to see what she dreaded the most. Yes, yes, it was him…Rocky the Rooster!

Rocky was easy to spot. He was larger than the others…taller than the others…and meaner, oh yes, much meaner than any of the others. He strutted across the coop proudly with his chest out and comb perched high in the air, bobbing as he walked.

Rocky wasn't just one to be feared. He was the meanest, double-winged, scratchiest rooster that ever roosted in the hen house. The other chickens waited on him wing and foot. When Rocky entered the food area, all the others backed up and allowed a wide area for Rocky to scratch.

Rocky looked to be in a particularly bad mood. He swaggered over to the gaggling hens. Without as much as a peep, he pecked at some of the smaller chickens feeding on the ground, sending them into a frenzy of flapping. They all scurried about in fear, running this way and that, bumping heads as feathers flew about the yard.

They were hungry, but when Rocky was around, he had all the lunch he wanted. Anytime Rocky wanted the thatch, Rocky got the thatch. It didn't matter if the others were hungry, he would take anyone's lunch. When a smaller chicken pecked too close to his thatch, Rocky taught him a lesson and knocked him to the ground.

The little chicken got up, dusted himself off, and quietly tip-toed over to the courtyard next to two cats. Rocky the Rooster was a bully!

Across the meadow perched on the fence posts, sat the cats twitching their tails and warming themselves in the sun. From a distance they looked peaceful and calm, but upon drawing closer to the felines, conversations could be heard. Not just ordinary boasting but big, bountiful, buoyant boasting.

"I am the best at cat games," meowed Meme.

"I am the best at catching mice the fastest. I am the best at tackling a ball of yarn, and I am the best at peering around corners and pouncing on prey. In fact, I'm pretty much the best hunter in the barnyard!" Meme exclaimed.

"Well, look at those cats over there," pawed Patches, as she pointed at the other fence posts. "They can't do the things that WE can do."

And the two meowed and purred, meowed and purred, purred and meowed. They puffed themselves up and tore others down with their words. They complained about the other cats loud enough for them to hear. No other cat could do things as well as they could, and they let them know it.

Even words can bully others, and these two confident cats had plenty of words to say that were hurtful to those around them, and hurt them they did—it made all the other cats stay very quiet about the things they could do.

Meme grew tired of hearing herself talk, so with her head held high, she padded away from the others. She used her cat instincts and sharp eyesight to peer out over the meadow. She spotted the sheep in the far meadow, lowing in the field.

There was one black sheep in the flock. The sheep with white wool were of far more value. Their wool was so white it sparkled in the sun and wasn't dingy or spotted. They knew that the farmer thought very highly of them. They gathered around the one black sheep, named Shelby, and spoke mean things to her.

"We are better than you, little black sheep," one shouted.

"We own better clothes, and we look nicer," poked another.

"We have more than you. In fact, we are the richest, coolest sheep in the count," another said.

Shelby bowed her head. She felt like a blob of chocolate pudding on your best shirt. She ran off to the hillside to be alone. Shelby liked the way she looked and couldn't help being a little different than the others. "I don't have as much hay and oats as the other sheep. I don't have pure, white wool like some of them but that doesn't mean I'm not important. My black wool can't be dyed, but I'm smart and nice to others. I can do the same things as white sheep. They are just bullies!" Shelby shouted.

The crows enjoyed the beautiful green meadows, the wheat fields blowing in the warm winds, and the spring flowers popping up out of the ground, beginning to bud and waiting to unfold. They circled far overhead, dipping their wings every now and then to hear a little clearer. As they swooped, they could see the horses, chickens, cats, and the sheep.

They glided over each section of the farm, watching everything. They watched the pushing, they watched the fighting, they heard the hurtful words, but they did nothing to help. The whole group went about their flying and let the bullying take place. They, too, were participating in bullying, because they ignored the bullying in the barnyard. They flew over to where the goats were locking horns and watched the kicking begin.

Over by the barn, the goats grazed and fought all the time. They threw a punch left and reached for their right. Their hooves were fast and they kicked and hit, kicked and hit, hit and kicked. They pushed each other around and didn't treat anyone nice. There was Bobby, Betty, and Belinda Sue. They were so mean, it's all they knew. They hurt others by fighting to get their own way. They weren't just billy goats, they were bully goats.

So how can this barnyard full of bullies be changed into a barnyard full of friends? How can we help the animals learn to get along as a group?

How can we STOP bullying?

Don't talk about others like the cats. Don't take things from others like the chickens. Don't pick on one another for what they wear—or the color of their skin or hair—like the sheep or the horses.

Treat others how you would like to be treated. Be kind to others and kindness will come back to you like the farmer, who plants seeds in the corn field. From the seeds, corn stalks grow out of the ground, which have ears of yummy, sweet, golden yellow corn. If you plant seeds of kindness, you will help kindness grow.

What is Bullying?

1. Speaking against others.
2. A group against one, intimidating others.
3. Taking things from others.
4. Causing physical harm.
5. Treating others poorly because they are different: clothes, possessions, skin, hair.
6. Using our voices, bodies, phones, computers, and other people to hurt someone.

STOP

So let's practice the BACK OFF BULLYING actions below:

S. T. O. P.

1. **S**peak kindly to others. Do not speak, write, or use the computer to hurt others.
2. Do not **T**ouch others to hurt them. Tell an adult if you see any bullying activity.
3. Remember to treat **O**thers like you would like to be treated.
4. Do not **P**articipate in the action of trying to make others do things they do not want to do.

Let's help make our school and homes a safer place
and LEAVE THE BULLIES IN THE BARNYARD!